Contents

KT-499-930

Using electricity

Have you ever thought about how much electricity you use in a normal day?

When you get up in the morning you might have toast cooked in a toaster. At school you will probably use a computer.

When you get home from school you may watch the television.

All of these machines use electricity and so do many more. Today, it would be hard for us to live without electricity.

£4.83

ELECTRICITY SUPPLY

s Nixon

FRANKLIN WATTS
LONDON · SYDNEY

First published in 2009 by
Franklin Watts
338 Euston Road
London NW1 3BH

Franklin Watts Australia
Level 17/207 Kent Street
Sydney NSW 2000

ISBN: 978 0 7496 8405 1

Dewey classification number: 333.793'2

A CIP catalogue record for this book is available
from the British Library.

Planning and production by Discovery Books Limited
Editor: James Nixon
Designer: Ian Winton
Illustrations: Stefan Chabluk
Commissioned photography: Bobby Humphrey

Photographs: Discovery Picture Library: pp. 15 bottom (Chris Fairclough), 17 bottom (Rachel
Tisdale); Getty Images: p. 11 bottom (Charles Thatcher); Istockphoto.com: pp. 6 top (Rob Cruse),
6 bottom (Jason Lugo), 7 top, 7 middle (Arthur Fatykhov), 7 bottom (Matjaz Boncina), 8 bottom
right (Yuriy Tuchkov), 9 both, 12 bottom (Alan Tobey), 13 (Rolf Fischer), 14 (Pavle Marjanovic),
15 top (Brian Jackson), 15 middle, 16 (Krzysztof Slusarczyk), 17 top (Dan Brandenburg), 18
(Robert Asento), 19 top (Jenny Hill), 19 bottom (Ian Hamilton), 26 top; Melanie Nixon: pp. 22
bottom, 25 bottom; Newscast/E.On UK: pp. 10 top, 11 top; NPower: p. 10 bottom; Shutterstock:
pp. 12 top (A. S. Zain).

Cover photos: Discovery Picture Library: bottom (Rachel Tisdale), Ian Winton: bottom right;
Shutterstock: top (Victor Soares), title background (Argus).

Printed in China

Franklin Watts is a division of Hachette Children's Books,
an Hachette Livre UK company.
www.hachettelivre.co.uk

Changing electricity

Electricity is a form of **energy**. Machines change electricity into different kinds of energy.

Electric cookers produce heat energy to cook food.

Microwave

Light bulb

Pembroke Branch Tel. 6689575

Light bulbs need electricity to produce light energy.

Stereos and MP3 players change electricity into sound energy. Food mixers change electricity into movement energy.

Stereo

Types of electricity

The electricity in your home flows along metal wires to every light switch and socket. This type of electricity, which is carried from one place to another, is called **current electricity**.

Battery power

A battery can be used to produce current electricity. Chemicals in the battery react with each other and create a small electric current. Batteries are usually used in smaller, portable gadgets, such as torches or mobile phones.

Where does electricity come from?

Large machines in your home need much more power than a battery can provide. They use the supply of electricity in the wall sockets. Do you know where this electricity comes from and how it gets to your home? This book will tell you how your electricity supply works.

Muking electricity

The electricity needed to power your home is **generated** in large buildings called power stations.

Turning the turbines

At the power station a fuel such as coal, oil or gas is burned to boil water. This water turns into **steam**, which then blasts out in a jet ⸻ ⸻ huge wheel called a **turbine**. The turbine is connected ⸻ generator. The ⸻erator converts ⸻e movement of the ⸻rbine into a current ⸻f electrical energy.

Turbines

Cooling it down

Beside the power station are a number of huge towers that look like giant chimneys. These are called cooling towers. They collect the steam that has been used in the power station and cool it down.

My name is Steve
I look after the machinery that generates electricity. I start and stop the generators depending on the amount of electricity we need to make. I also keep a record of any breakdowns or repair work that has taken place.

Fossil fuels

In the UK, the most common fuels burned in power stations are natural gas and coal. These fuels are called **fossil fuels**.

Out of the ground

Like fossils, fossil fuels take millions of years to form. They formed under the ground long ago from the rotting remains of dead plants and animals.

Coal

Pump

Pipes

Workers reach layers of coal by mining (above) and natural gas by drilling wells and pumping it up into pipelines on the surface (left

Polluting the air

Coal and gas are useful 'high-energy' fuels. However when they burn they give off gases and smoke that cause pollution. We need to find cleaner, alternative ways to make our electricity.

Nuclear

In the future more of our electricity will be generated in nuclear power stations. Nuclear power is made from a metal called uranium. In some types of uranium tiny particles inside can be split apart to make a **nuclear reaction**. These reactions produce enormous amounts of heat. This is used to make steam in nuclear power stations. Nuclear power is clean but can be dangerous if something goes wrong.

Reactor

▲ **Nuclear reactions take place inside a thick steel reactor.**

Other sources of energy

If we keep using more and more fossil fuels to make electricity they will soon run out.

Electricity companies are now using sources of energy that will last forever, such as water, wind or **solar** power. These **renewable** sources of energy do not produce harmful gases either.

Water power

Electricity can be made at a hydro-electric power plant. Here, water is held back behind a dam to form a huge **reservoir** (below).

Water is allowed to rush through pipes to a turbine, which turns to generate electricity.

Hydro-electric power plant

Wind power

Another energy source is the wind. Wind farms have been built where huge turbines are turned by the wind to make electricity (right).

Mini turbine

Do it yourself

Some homes make their own electricity using renewable energy sources. Mini wind turbines can be fitted onto the roof. Some homes have solar panels attached to the roof. The panels take in energy from the Sun and use it to heat water or create electricity.

Solar panels

Transporting electricity

How does electricity made in power stations get to the sockets in your home and every other home?

Pylons and cables

From the power station electricity is moved all over the country using a huge network of cables. This system is called the **National Grid**. Sometimes the cables are held high above the ground by pylons. In towns and cities the cables are usually buried deep underground.

Power cuts

Bad weather can cause damage to power lines. This may cause a power cut. In storms, high winds and falling trees can pull cables down. Power lines are extremely dangerous. Stay far away from them.

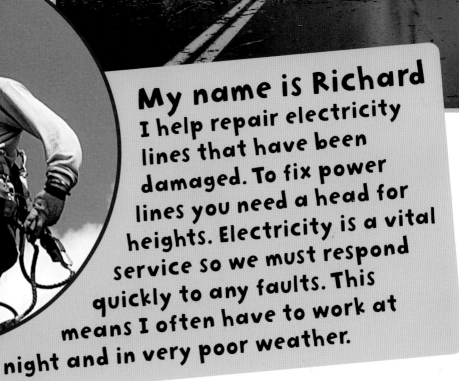

My name is Richard
I help repair electricity lines that have been damaged. To fix power lines you need a head for heights. Electricity is a vital service so we must respond quickly to any faults. This means I often have to work at night and in very poor weather.

Lowering the voltage

Electricity from power stations has a long way to travel. So it is pushed out at a high **voltage**. The voltage is the force of the electricity and is measured in volts. The voltage of electricity that runs between pylons can be as high as 500,000 volts.

Transformer

Transformers

Before the electricity reaches your home it has to be turned into a lower, safer voltage (around 230 volts) by a **transformer**. If the voltage were any higher, all your electrical machines might blow up.

Substations

The transformers are often behind high fences in substations. You may have seen a **substation** near your house. Substations are very dangerous places and you should never go inside them or play near them.

Substation

DANGER OF DEATH

Danger signs

This is the warning sign that you will see near substations and power lines. High-voltage electricity is so powerful that it can jump and kill you even if you don't touch anything. So when you see this sign, remember: keep out and keep your distance.

Once the electricity cable comes into your home it goes to a panel called a consumer unit (see page 22). In the unit is the mains switch where you can turn the electricity on and off. From the unit wires are carried through the walls, under the floors and around the ceilings to different parts of your home.

Electricity cable

Circuits

There is usually a set of wires for the light switches upstairs and downstairs. A further set of wires carry electricity to the sockets in the walls. Each set of wires forms a circuit. A circuit is a loop that electricity can flow around. There is a switch for each circuit in the consumer unit. The electric cooker and the water heater have their own circuits, too.

Electricity around the home

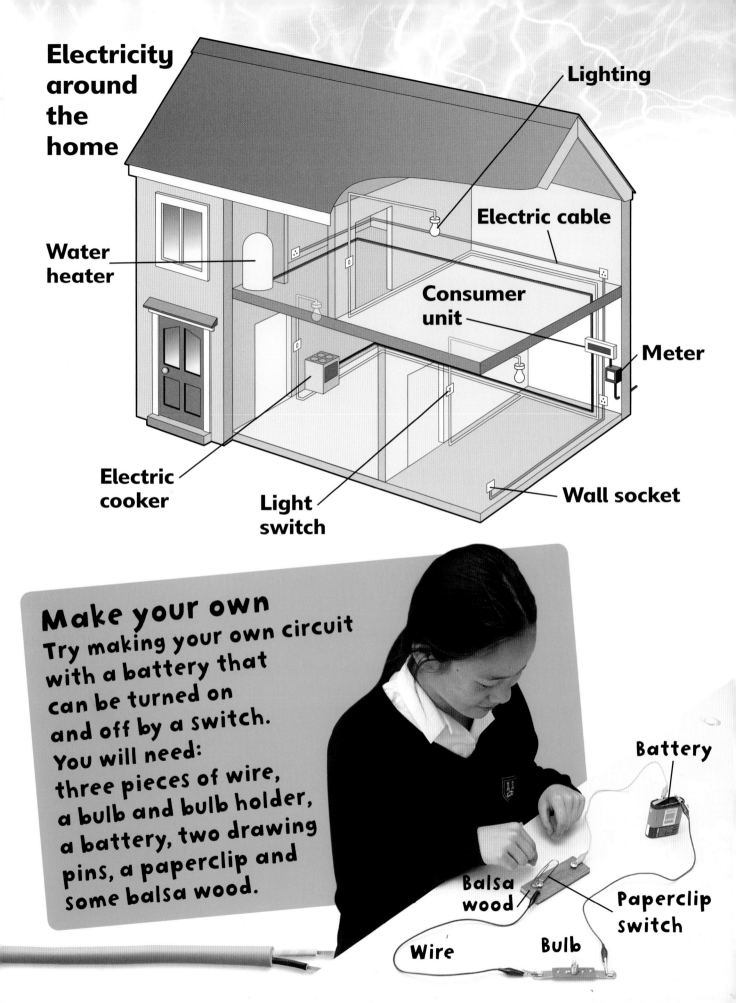

Lighting

Electric cable

Water heater

Consumer unit

Meter

Electric cooker

Light switch

Wall socket

Make your own

Try making your own circuit with a battery that can be turned on and off by a switch. You will need: three pieces of wire, a bulb and bulb holder, a battery, two drawing pins, a paperclip and some balsa wood.

Battery

Balsa wood

Paperclip switch

Wire

Bulb

Keeping Safe

Electricity can be very dangerous. If it flows through your body it will give you an electric shock that can kill you. Do not touch wires in the home that are uncovered.

Pull switch

You must follow these rules to stay safe from electricity:

- Never stick anything into a socket other than a plug.
- Do not poke inside appliances.
- Never use electrical devices near water.
- Do not touch light switches or plugs with wet hands. For safety, pull switches are often used in bathrooms.

Safety devices

The switches in the consumer unit, called trip switches, turn the electricity off automatically if there is a fault.

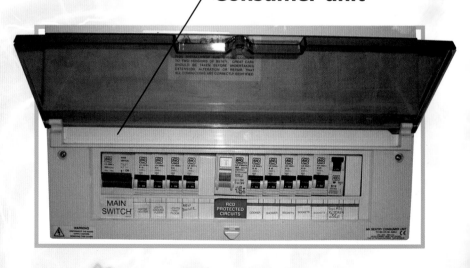

Consumer unit

Inside a plug

Plugs carry electricity safely from the sockets to the machines that you use. Inside the plug are three wires and a safety device called a **fuse**. The wire inside a fuse gets hot and breaks if you plug in a faulty appliance. This cuts off the supply of electricity and prevents a fire breaking out.

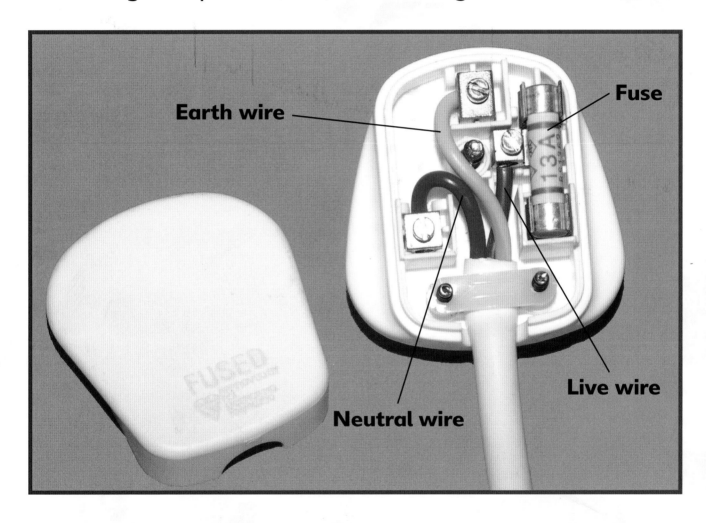

The green and yellow wire (earth wire) is a safety wire that allows electricity to pass into the ground (not into you) when there is a fault. The blue and brown wires carry electricity.

Meters and bills

As electricity enters your home it passes through an electricity meter. A spinning dial in the meter measures the amount of electricity your home uses. The more electricity being used the faster the dial spins.

Spinning dial

kWh

7 3 3 1 5

10000 1000 100 10 1

Numbers

Reading the meter

With an adult find the meter for your house. It might be on a wall outside or in a cupboard inside.

Look at the row of numbers. These give a reading, which tells you how much electricity you have used.

Every so often a meter reader from the electricity company comes to look at the reading. The company then knows how much to charge you and will send a bill (right).

Amount to pay

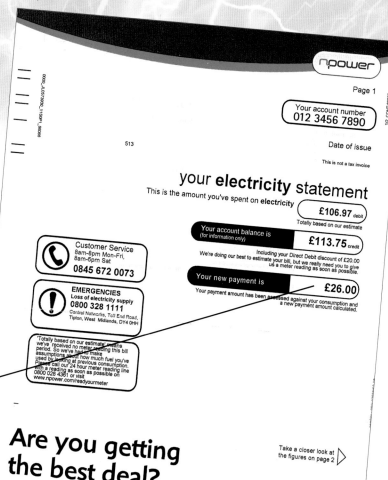

npower

Page 1

Your account number
012 3456 7890

513

Date of issue

This is not a tax invoice

your **electricity** statement
This is the amount you've spent on electricity

£106.97 debit

Totally based on our estimate

Your account balance is
(for information only)

£113.75 credit

Including your Direct Debit discount of £20.00
We're doing our best to estimate your bill, but we really need you to give us a meter reading as soon as possible.

Your new payment is

£26.00

Your payment amount has been assessed against your consumption and a new payment amount calculated.

Customer Service
8am-8pm Mon-Fri,
8am-6pm Sat
0845 672 0073

EMERGENCIES
Loss of electricity supply
0800 328 1111
Central Networks, Toll End Road,
Tipton, West Midlands, DY4 0HH

'Totally based on our estimate' means we've 'received no meter reading this bill period. So we've had to make assumptions about how much fuel you've used by looking at previous consumption. Please call our 24 hour meter reading line with a reading as soon as possible on 0800 028 4361 or visit www.npower.com/readyourmeter

Are you getting the best deal?

Take your gas and electricity from us, pay by monthly Direct Debit throughout the year and you could qualify for an £80 discount*.

Call us for more information on 0800 316 0609†

Take a closer look at the figures on page 2 ▷

* Terms and Conditions apply, subject to availability.
† Calls may be monitored and recorded for training and security purposes. Calls from BT landlines will be charged up to 5p per minute. The price of calls may vary with other operators. Please check with your operator for exact charges.

Electricity is supplied by Npower Limited (Registered No. 3653277). Registered in England and Wales. Registered Of... SN5 6PB.

BM36

Card

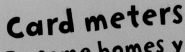

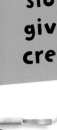

Card meters
In some homes you pay for electricity before you use it. You take a card into a shop and put electricity credit onto it. The card then slots into your meter and will give you electricity until the credit on the card runs out.

Saving electricity

The less electricity we use the less it will cost. So it is a good idea to try and use as little electricity as possible.

Looking after the environment

We also know that electricity is produced by burning fossil fuels, which pollutes the

air. Every time you turn on the lights you are creating a little pollution even though you can't see it. By using less electricity you will be keeping the environment cleaner. Here are some tips on saving electricity:

• If you replace light bulbs with energy-saving light bulbs you will use up to four times less electricity.

• Make sure machines are switched off completely when you are not using them. A television that is on standby is still using electricity.

• Instead of using your tumble dryer, washing can be hung up to dry.

• When you boil water in the kettle only fill it up with the amount of water that you are going to use. Otherwise you are wasting electricity.

Glossary

Credit The amount of money added in to an account to pay for a service, such as electricity supply or mobile phone calls.

Current electricity The movement of electricity through a wire.

Energy Something that makes things work. Electricity is a form of energy.

Fossil fuels Fuel found in the ground, such as coal and gas, that formed from the remains of animals and plants that lived millions of years ago.

Fuse A safety device that melts and breaks an electric circuit if the current is above a safe level.

Generated Produced a form of energy, such as electricity.

National Grid The nationwide network of wires and cables that carry electricity around the country.

Nuclear reaction The huge amounts of heat released when tiny particles of certain types of uranium are split apart.

React If one substance reacts with another when mixed, a chemical change takes place.

Renewable Describes an energy source that will not run out, such as the wind or the Sun.

Reservoir A lake used for creating hydro-electricity or storing water before it is supplied to people.

Solar power Describes energy that comes from the Sun.

Static electricity A build-up of electric charge caused by certain objects rubbing together. Static means not moving.

Steam The hot vapour produced when water is boiled. It looks like a white mist.

Substation The part of the National Grid where transformers lower the voltage before electricity is supplied to your home.

Transformer A device used for changing the voltage of an electric current.

Turbine A machine that is turned by the force of steam, wind or water.

Voltage The measure of the force of an electric current.

Further information

Books

Charging About: The Story of Electricity, Jacqui Bailey and Matthew Lilly, 2004 (A & C Black Publishers)

Electricity (Amazing Science), Sally Hewitt, 2006 (Wayland)

Electricity (I Know That), Claire Llewellyn, 2003 (Franklin Watts)

Electricity: Turn it on, Wendy Sadler, 2005 (Raintree)

Websites

www.ngfl-cymru.org.uk/vtc/using_electricity/eng/Introduction
This site contains activities that show you how we use electricity in the home.

www.firstschoolyears.com/science/electricity/interactive/ electricityquiz.swf
Test your knowledge with this electricity quiz.

www.edfenergy.com/powerup
This website tells you more about our electricity supply and is packed with interactive games and activities.

Note to parents and teachers: Every effort has been made by the Publishers to ensure that these websites are suitable for children, that they are of the highest educational value, and that they contain no inappropriate or offensive material. However, because of the nature of the Internet, it is impossible to guarantee that the contents of these sites will not be altered. We strongly advise that Internet access is supervised by a responsible adult.

Index